30% Fat What's That?

A Simple Answer to a Complex Question

by Patricia Ormsby Borer

Editor: John J. Borer, Jr.

Cover and illustrations by Anne Cornell, Art Director

Technical Advisor: Sandy Segien, R. D., B.S.

Book Design by Patricia Ormsby Borer

Published in Rancho Santa Fe, California, United States of
America by Vitaerobics, Inc. 1987

First Printing May 1987
Second Printing August 1987

The information in this book is not intended as medical
advice. It is solely informational and educational. The
reader should consult a medical or health professional
if one is needed.

Library of Congress Catalog Card Number: 87-81333

ISBN 0-9618845-0-9

Dedicated to God who gives us life and the faith, guidance, courage and strength to live it.

To Dr. Kenneth Cooper and Covert Bailey who by their teachings and dedication have provided ways to improve the quality of life.

To John who has taken their teachings and proven WHERE THERE IS A WILL, THERE IS A WAY.

We challenge you to B. A. FAT FINDER™ for three months. Chances are your weight will soon be watching itself. Write and tell us your success story. Once a month we will draw a winner and award one of the books we have listed.

VITAEROBICS, INC.
4403 Manchester Ave. - Suite 107
Encinitas, CA 92067
(619) 753-9171

We know you have TIPS and RECIPES you would like to share. Send them to us for publication and we will enter your name in a monthly drawing for a cookbook

B. A. FATFINDER™

Lodl (LDL) is the "bad guy" destroying cardiovascular fitness in bodies that are fed too much fat. You can tell him by his nasty scowl.

Hidl (HDL) is the "good guy". His mission is to destroy Lodls before their damage is done. HE'S THE ONE WITH THE BIG SMILE.

It has long been said that necessity is the mother of invention. The FAT FINDER is the direct result of such a need!

At age 53, my husband suffered a silent heart attack and had a quadruple coronary bypass. This may come as a shock, but he had been waiting for this to happen. Even more shocking, he had lived most of his life making certain it WOULD happen. He had ample warning. His father had a fatal heart attack at age 58. His younger brother had a severe heart attack at age 46. John himself had been diagnosed as hypertensive at the "tender" age of 27. To add to the "downside" of this scenario, 3 of his father's brothers had coronary heart disease at early ages.

John was a prime candidate for the disease
- in the VERY HIGH RISK CATEGORY! He
didn't deny it but rather took a
fatalistic attitude. With such a strong
family history of the disease he refused
to believe he had any control over the
situation. Doctors prescribed
medications, and he took them. They
never talked about the benefits that could
flow from a life-style change or
modification. This was difficult for me
to understand, and I was amazed at their
reaction and lack of concern - their
apparent complacency. On more than one
occasion I tried to talk to John's
doctors. I would be told he could lose a
few pounds but that it is hard to change
what a person does and how he lives.
While he resented the side effects of the
medications, the morning pill ritual
became a regular part of his life and he
accepted it.

The extra twenty pounds became a too
abundant part of his life, as did the long
corporate-suite hours with their unending
stress and pressures. The combination
always takes its toll, and what was
happening was obvious to me. Again
becoming frightened, I contacted the
doctor who tried to ENLIGHTEN me by
explaining that this was the picture of a
"successful" TYPE A personality. Lit-

tle consolation to me who knew the life of someone I loved was at stake.

Actually, John was more fortunate than most when his heart attack struck. While it was "silent," it was not fatal. It is called "silent" because there is no pain associated with it. I am certain it happened on an airplane, as he returned from Washington, D.C. at the end of a week of "adrenalin flowing" meetings. He boarded the plane, had a drink to relax, and the "silent killer" took over. I knew when I met him at the airport that something had happened. His face was drawn and his color ashen. I was in nurse's training long before the fancy machines we have today. We were trained to look for signs and symptoms. I knew IT had happened. Of course he said he felt fine - maybe a little tired. The next day he thought he had a touch of the flu. He complained of a "little sour taste," which often accompanies this type of heart attack. He was too busy for the next few weeks to go to the doctor, but when he went the EKG confirmed what I had known all along. A heart attack had taken place.

After a battery of tests, bypass surgery was recommended and immediately scheduled. The operation was successful - a quick fix allowing John to make light of the experience, and not seem to take the state of his health too seriously.

He did start a program of vigorous walking an hour a day, which seemed to be as good for him psychologically as physically. The doctors insisted he go back on beta blocker medication. After about a year the walking got lost in a "busy" schedule, and he was back on his suicidal course. It was an attitude of eat, drink and be merry today - so what if we die tomorrow! If we die we die. The following years were repeat performances. Depression resulting from the medication, as well as the physical deterioration, were evident - a constant worry to me. I realize now they were even more frightening for John but that he felt helpless. There was a whole personality change.

By late 1984, I decided I was witnessing a case of what doctors mean when they say, "the surgery was successful but we lost the patient." I knew time was running out. In early 1985 I started a more urgent search for an answer. I had heard of "Pritikin" but had not been able to interest John. He had the same negative reaction to various other Southern California programs.

I am an investigative person by nature and enjoy learning. I have always been very active, and have not had a weight problem since losing my "baby fat" in my teens. I shopped for and prepared over 200,000 meals in raising our 9 children. (This doesn't include the "strange faces" that usually pulled-up a chair at our table.)

The more I learned about aerobic exercise, and the theory of "overweight" vs "overfat," the more I was convinced of the close relation between these terms and the cardiovascular system; and in particular how relative they were to my husband's well-being. Being FIT not FAT was the answer. CUT THE FAT OUT - PUT THE EXERCISE IN.

It was in this learning process that the FAT FINDER was conceived. Since I have always had the "head for figures" in our family, it was my job to "figure the % of fat." While John's results on 20-25% fat intake were great - 20lb weight loss, 20-30 point drop in blood pressure and a 20% lower cholesterol reading - I was getting tired of being a human calculator. Since I have never been a "morning person," figuring the fat was not a great way to start the day. One morning, as I tried to figure the fat from the label on a box of cereal, I said, "WHAT WE NEED IS" and described an easy way to arrive at the answer. A telephone call to our engineer son-in-law, a mathematics whiz, made the simplified calculation a reality, and we now have the FAT FINDER.

USE IT AND LEARN AND YOU WILL GREATLY IMPROVE THE QUALITY OF YOUR LIFE. I have seen it yield fantastic results. I know it will do the same for you.

SOBERING THOUGHT:
An "over-fat body" is an overworked body.

BOTTOM LINE:
TRY THE **NO DRUG THERAPY** FIRST -
B. A. FAT FINDER!

SERIOUS BUSINESS

Cholesterol and fat have been the focal point of many studies and the conclusions are unanimous that MORE IS NOT BETTER. The higher the cholesterol reading, the greater the risk of coronary heart disease. Now that we have been presented with the facts, we should heed them. This is serious business...you have only one thing to lose...YOUR LIFE! We must position ourselves to make educated judgements and choices; to take responsibility to the extent we can, and to care. I believe all of us do. So don't wait for the doctor of your choice to give you a pill and think all your problems will be solved. Remember, GOD HELPS THOSE WHO HELP THEMSELVES. Be responsive when studies tell you diet modification and 3-4 hours of aerobic exercise each week make a difference...
...THEY DO! The associations are clear--high cholesterol levels and coronary heart disease; low cholesterol and good cardiovascular health. YOU CAN CHOOSE TO IMPROVE THE QUALITY OF YOUR LIFE.

The information flow being presented in the areas of nutrition, exercise and wellness is exciting and should be seen as an opportunity and a challenge. Don't let another day pass without saying to yourself..."I cannot change yesterday, I can only live for today, and plan for tomorrow."

Using the Fat Finder will help you plan for a healthier tomorrow.

SOBERING QUESTION:
Are you going to stand by and do nothing while "greasy" cholesterol clogs your "plumbing"?

BOTTOM LINE:
FAT CAN BE HAZARDOUS TO YOUR HEALTH!

Learn to be a wise shopper. Compare brands, fat content, nutrients and calories. Know the facts - do not rely on catchy words like light - lite and natural. Learn to choose your calories wisely. Get more and better nutrient value - money is important but your health is what really counts.

If you don't know, or can't determine the content of a food, don't buy it.

Cut down on sugar by using fresh fruit juices when baking or cooking.

Put fresh fruit through food processor, then use it fresh or freeze in bag for later use.

When you cook dried fruit remember it has 3 times the sugar concentration of fresh fruit. Before cooking soak and drain water twice. Save the juice and use for flavor when cooking other foods. It is excellent used in pancakes, waffles or muffins. It also can be used with cinnamon, almond, vanilla or maple for adding flavor to hot cereals.

30% FAT...WHAT'S THAT?

We are constantly bombarded with information about nutrition and related health problems experienced by Americans. This is as it should be. Wellness should be our No. 1 priority. A good health maintenance program is like having money in the bank, or an extra insurance policy. Something we can do for ourselves and over which we can have some control.

Of primary concern here is the overconsumption of fat. The average American diet reportedly consists of 42% fat; and, while our diet should be less than 30%, even this number is somewhat arbitrary. Admittedly, the presently recommended goal of less than 30% is a vast improvement over 42%. It is generally agreed that 20% would be more ideal, but that our culture would find this adjustment too extreme. Maybe "extreme" depends on your point of view...what is "extreme" if your well being depends on it?

A diet of 30% fat is not as difficult to accomplish as to understand. It would be nice if "fat" came tied in a nice neat package marked "FAT," but it does not. Some high-fat foods are actually packaged/ marketed in almost that way, with clever

packaging and logo to give eye appeal.
Since fat itself has little or no taste,
it is masked with other "goodies." In
reality, what is presented as HEAVENLY
MELT-IN-YOUR-MOUTH is DEADLY DELIGHT!

We all know the food we eat, as well as
the energy we expend, is measured in
calories. The ideal is to match intake
and output on a daily basis, but this
seems to be an instance where ideal ex-
ists only in our minds - not in reality.
Many of us take in far more calories than
we use. These are then stored in/on our
bodies as fat. We have no trouble finding
that fat!

In a diet consisting of 30% fat your fat
calories cannot exceed 30% of your total
calorie intake. If that intake is 2000
calories, the fat calories should not be
more than 600. (Since each gram of fat
has 9 calories, this would allow about 66
grams of fat.) To achieve this goal we
must limit our overall diet to less than
30% fat. We must learn to compensate for
eating those foods high in fat content
(over 30%) by eating more items well below
the 30% level, and some with no fat at
all. Given the number of fat grams, the
FAT FINDER tells this percentage instantly. When we are tempted and go over the
limit, it enables us to adjust to less
than 30% the next meal or the next day.

SOBERING FACT:
An enlightened mind means more responsibility. THE BUCK STOPS HERE!

BOTTOM LINE:
It's hard to find fat on a FAT FINDER!

BE AN INSTANT EXPERT

THE FAT FINDER IS THE SIMPLE, QUICK, ACCURATE ANSWER TO A COMPLEX QUESTION. It does in an instant exactly what it was designed to do...it tells the percentage of fat in food. By aligning two given numbers (total calories and grams of fat) you are shown in the window the percentage of fat contained in a given amount of food. The FAT FINDER does this by taking the given **NUMBER of GRAMS OF FAT, multiplying** them **by 9** (there are 9 calories in 1 gram of fat) and **dividing** this **by the TOTAL NUMBER OF CALORIES**.

Example:
1 serving of XYZ has 150 calories
1 serving of XYZ has   9 grams of fat
TURN the wheel until the 9 on the inner circle is in line with the 150 on the outer circle. The answer in the window shows that XYZ contains 54% fat per serving. (To check the accuracy of the FAT FINDER, use a pencil and paper, do it in your head or get out your expensive calculator.) Multiply 9X9 and divide by 150. The answer should be 54%.

The percentage of **fat in food** can be calculated instantly when you are given "Nutrition Information" on the labeling/ package of an item.

EXAMPLE:
NUTRITION INFORMATION
      Per Serving
Calories.........150
Protein...........4 grams
Carbohydrate......14 grams
Fat.............. 9 grams
Sodium..........280 milligrams
Potassium....... 70 milligrams

The percentage of fat in a recipe can be calculated instantly when the number of grams of fat contained in the recipe are listed - usually at the end of the recipe instructions. Although full, complicated nutrient information may be helpful for other aspects of nutrition, all that is needed for our purposes is the total number of calories and the number of grams of fat in a given serving.

EXAMPLE:
EACH PANCAKE: 115 calories, 4 Grams FAT
or
Per serving:
430 calories; 52 gm protein; 8.5 gm fat; 24.8 gm carbohydrate; 6.4 gm fiber; 105 mg cholesterol; 3.7mg iron; 125mg sodium; 1050mg potassium; etc.

More and more recipes are listing this information and I believe this practice will increase with public demand.   Try to select cookbooks and culinary magazines that include this information with the recipes, as recipes can tend to have hidden fat and cholesterol. Two eggs here, a half a cup of butter there and a cup of sour cream along the way!

Additionally, the percentage of fat can be calculated in any food when you know the number of grams of fat. PENNINGTON AND CHURCH'S FOOD VALUES OF PORTIONS COMMONLY USED is an excellent source of this information.

EXAMPLE:
Fish - Halibut, Atlantic/Pacific, broiled
3 1/2 oz   214 calories 8.8 gm Fat
Line up 8.8 on the small wheel with 214 on the large wheel and the window will show 37%.   Likewise:
Hamburger, lean, cooked
1 patty 140 calories 3.4 gm Fat
Your Fat Finder instantly reveals a percentage of fat of 22%.

For items having more than 600 calories, divide the number of calories and the grams of fat in half and find the percentage for those amounts. The percentage will be the same for the larger amounts.

SOBERING DISCOVERY:
Calculate the percentage of fat in foods
presently in your cupboard.

BOTTOM LINE:
Now you are an expert and the fun begins!
B.A. FAT FINDER.

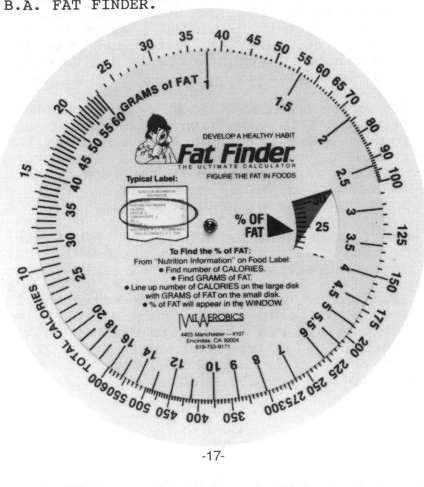

For egg substitutes use Ener-G Egg Replacer, Egg Beaters, or Featherweight Egg Magic.

Use moistened oats (oat meal) when baking, or in waffles or pancakes. Place oats in plastic bag, add warm water and soak for five minutes. Punch holes in bag to drain water before using.

Use carob or cocoa POWDER for chocolate flavor. Both are high in potassium and low in sodium. Carob does not have the stimulant (caffeine) present in cocoa. Both are to be avoided in the form of bits or candy, as those are usually high in palm, palm kernel or coconut oil.

Use Butter Buds as substitute for butter or margarine. Butter Buds have sodium but less than salted butter or margarine.

Slice water bagels very thin and place in 250 degree oven until crisp. Place low fat cocktail rye or pumpernickel on cookie sheet in 250 degree oven until crisp. Turn off oven and let sit until cool. Keep in plastic bag for snacking.

FIND THE FAT...IT'S IN THE LABEL

We wouldn't think of buying a new car without reading the sticker. We read all the literature available from the manufacturer concerning its mechanical features. Of particular concern, are the safety features. We can't be too cautious. Further, we would not spend our money for clothes that didn't fit properly; so we look for the correct size. We are interested in the fabric content and care instructions. Certain brand names mean quality. And oh yes, the designer label! Think of this "quality control" the next time you steer your cart through the grocery store!

LEARN TO BE A LABEL READER

The most important labels you will ever read are on the foods you eat. Knowing what this printed information means is vital to your health and well being. There are two types of information given, "Nutrition Information" and "Ingredients.

"NUTRITION INFORMATION" is listed as follows:

>   PER SERVING
>   SERVING SIZE
>   SERVINGS PER CONTAINER
>   . . . .

CALORIES
PROTEIN
CARBOHYDRATES
FAT
SODIUM

A word of caution......note the serving size carefully. Many times, particularly in high calorie items, the serving size is a considerably smaller portion than we would consider a usual serving. I recently picked up a box of cereal and the calories didn't seem too high, until I looked at the size of the serving. A one ounce serving (1/5 cup) had 110 calories. A reasonable portion would be 2-3 ounces, or 330 calories, WITHOUT milk or fruit. You would expect ice cream to be high in calories, but might be a little shocked to find a serving size listed at a scant 1/2 cup. When was the last time you ate 1/2 cup of ice cream?

Along with the number of calories per serving, NUTRITION INFORMATION tells the number of grams of carbohydrate, protein, and fat, and milligrams of sodium per serving. More and more, as its importance is being recognized, the number of milligrams of potassium is also being included. <u>Since the object of label reading is to keep fat intake to less than 30% of your diet,</u> THIS IS THE ONLY NUTRIENT with which we will be concerned here. However, for the sake of knowledge, you should know how to figure the carbohydrate and protein calories as well, and should constantly be aware of sodium and potassium intake.

Carbohydrates and protein have 4 calories per gram. FAT has 9 calories per gram- 225% as dense. This difference, plus the chemical composition of fat, explains why we are so fat as a nation. We consume too many fat calories. To emphasize the difference, you should know that a cup of flour has 400 calories, a cup of sugar 800 calories and a cup of oil 2000 calories!

It is also important, when label reading, to note if the food requires additions before consumption. This is necessary to figure the percentage of fat with the additions, as it will be eaten.

Now let's calculate:
EXAMPLE:

NUTRITION INFORMATION
PER SERVING
Serving Size 1/2 cup
Servings Per Container 6

	Mix to Make 1 Serving	Prepared Pudding Using Whole Milk
CALORIES	80	160*
PROTEIN	0	4
CARBOHYDATE	21gm	27gm
FAT	1gm	5gm
SODIUM	140mg	200mg

*save 30 calories/serving - use skim milk

To figure the percentage of fat:
Multiply the number of grams of fat x 9 calories = total number of fat calories.

```
FAT 1gm                          5gm
  x 9calories               x 9calories
    9calories                 45calories
```

Next, divide the number of fat calories by the total number of calories = percentage of fat.

9 divided by 80=11% /45 divided by 160=28%

(To check the math, take your FAT FINDER and align 5 grams of fat on the small wheel with 160 calories on the large one.) The FAT FINDER does it all in an instant!

Unfortunately, "NUTRITION INFORMATION" is not required by law, and some manufacturers do not include it on their labels. I would strongly urge you not to buy products without this information. You must have it to make an intelligent decision. If consumers refuse to buy products that do not list this information, manufacturers will become more aware of its importance and provide it. If you do not know the exact content, you should not take the risk. Find an alternative.

INGREDIENTS

Ingredients are listed on the package in order of descending proportions, that is the ingredient of the greatest amount is listed first and the least amount listed last. Of utmost importance in this list is the type of fat contained in the product. Remember, hydrogenated, and partially hydrogenated oil, no matter what kind, means saturated fat, as does the phrase "assorted palm, coconut or other hydrogenated oil." These are oils that are considered detrimental to your health but are used because of their low cost. Manufacturers will get the message only if we refuse to buy products that are hazardous to our health. FIND A SUBSTITUTE!

If "Nutrition Information" is not given on a product, you can request it from the manufacturer. The following would be sufficient:

>"For good health reasons, I am interested in the nutritional content of the foods I (my family) eat. Please advise as to the "Nutrition Information" figures for your ------."

For a quick reply, I would enclose a self addressed, stamped envelope.

SOBERING THOUGHT:
High fat foods will be a minute in your mouth, an hour in your stomach, and forever on your hips!
BOTTOM LINE:
READ LABELS - B. A. FAT FINDER, NOT A RISK TAKER!

Find a store that carries plain, non-fat yogurt. Keep it on hand and use as you would sour cream.

Mix plain, non-fat yogurt with natural (no sugar or artificial sweeteners added) jams and jellies for use on pancakes and waffles. Delicious and no fat added.

For salad variety, try finely chopped broccoli with no fat salad dressing.

Try low calorie - low or no fat salad dressings. Estee Low Sodium - No Fat and Dieter's Gourmet Low Oil Italian or Creamy Garlic dressings are both packaged in individual packets easily carried in a plastic bag for pocket or purse...great for dining out. They are also ideal for marinating chicken or meat. Hollywood Lite Way Italian - No Oil Dressing (dry mix - add vinegar and water) is good for use at home. Especially tasty when used to marinate garbanzo beans for salads.

Non-fat yogurt, with salsa or picante sauce, makes an excellent vegetable or chip dip - also tasty over chicken when baking or broiling.

YOU CAN MAKE A DIFFERENCE

History, some of it good and some of it not so good, is repeated when we are born. Nevertheless, it is history and we cannot change it. This is the part of us we call heredity. These are the givens with which we must live. Each of us has a mother and a father, and from them comes our basic physical and psychological being. There are dominant genes and recessive genes, and even our parents have no control over how they are mixed to form a new being. This is up to God, who gives us life. Having given birth nine times, this is still the miracle of miracles. I look at my children as different masterpieces by the same artists. From a glance you can tell they are from the same mold because the familial resemblances are very strong. We recently had the marvelous opportunity of having four generations together - my mother, myself, a daughter and a granddaughter. The ages spanned 87 years. The physical characteristics were clearly evident. The threads of relationship (heredity) were obvious...seeing is believing.

While it is not obvious to the naked eye, we certainly have to believe the laws of genetics that tell us our physiology is just as related to our parents as our outward appearance. There are predisposed tendencies because we were born to certain parents. It is important to remember we are the combination of two people not related by blood. If both parents have a common trait or tendency it is going to be a very strong influence. If it is only one parent that has the trait the odds are in favor of dilution. As a child I was an asthmatic. This was not too surprising as my mother also had asthma. Neither of my sisters had the problem. One out of three, not bad. Only one of my children had the condition. One out of nine - even better.

In the case of cardiovascular disease, we are strongly warned that family history is the greatest single risk factor - one over which we have no control. We cannot change who our parents are and who we are. This presents a frightening scenario since none of us like to deal with our own mortality.

Deal with it we must. How we deal with it is a matter of choice. We can deny, which probably is the most pleasant in the short term; have a fatalistic approach which says "so what, we can't change it," or we can face reality and take responsibility for changing those risk factors we can change. We can decide to be our own best friend or our own worst enemy!

Have you ever thought about the statement
"Lookout for No. 1" or "Take care of
No.1?" Isn't that the Madison Avenue
approach to the supposedly good life?
Yet, when it comes to lifestyle, we tend
to think of what will gratify us now - not
what will be good for us in the long run.
This is what I call "instant insanity."

Don't be a victim of this attitude. Start influencing those factors over which you have control. The quality of your life is dependent on the effort you put forth day by day. If your nutrition habits need changing - begin the change today. If you are overweight - lose pounds. If you are a workaholic - slow down. If your stress level is continually in a state of "distress" - try several hours of biofeedback or learning relaxation techniques. Commit to a program of aerobic exercise 3-4 times a week. Find a new hobby or indulge in an old one. Don't find excuses in the heritage you can't change - take pride in working to change the odds.

SOBERING THOUGHT:
Each generation has responsibility to improve the quality of life.

BOTTOM LINE:
Faith and a strong will can move mountains and can overcome adversity.

Bake turkey breast for sandwiches. Remove skin before baking. Baste with a natural flavored seltzer or a mixture of half light fruit juice and half Perrier. Carbonation keeps meat moist while pulling out fat. Be aware that white meat has less cholesterol. Cook on rack. Do not let stand in its own juice.

Bake, broil, steam or poach meats and fish.

Do not add fats when preparing meats. Use teflon skillet when browning.

The higher the grade of meat, the more fat it will have. BE AWARE! Prime Grade has the most, Choice Grade less and Good Grade has least of all.

Cut down on portion sizes. Buy an accurate scale for weighing until you have enough practice to "guesstimate."

Shop for items as low in sodium and as high in potassium as possible.

A combination of rice and beans is an excellent source of protein and fiber.

TAKE THE HIGH ROAD

While volumes have been written about cholesterol, there are still many mysteries surrounding this fatty substance. It is agreed that cholesterol is a substance where LESS IS BETTER!

Cholesterol belongs to the sterol group of fats, a different class from saturated and unsaturated fats. Synthesized in our bodies, cholesterol is a vital substance of life. It is valuable in making cell membranes and Vitamin D. The liver uses cholesterol to produce bile acids which aid in digestion; certain other organs use cholesterol to manufacture hormones, the chemical substances that influence many bodily activities, including sex. The human liver manufactures all the cholesterol we need for such purposes. NOW FOR THE BAD NEWS...it is believed that saturated fat stimulates the liver to produce more cholesterol and that cholesterol clogs coronary arteries.

Cholesterol is transported through the body by attaching to proteins. These micro-packages of fat and protein called lipoproteins have been the subject of research in an effort to uncover the link between cholesterol and heart disease. Total blood cholesterol reflects the amount of cholesterol contained in several different types of lipoprotein, some "good" and some "bad".

"Bad," Low Density Lipoproteins, (LDL), in part destined for coronary arteries, bear a heavy burden of cholesterol. As cholesterol infiltrates the artery, scar tissue forms around it. The resulting "placques" increasingly block the artery, blood flow is diminished, and less oxygen is carried to the cells. The higher the LDL count, the more likely it is that large placques will form in coronary arteries, increasing the risk of coronary heart disease.

High Density Lipoproteins, (HDL), are the "good guys". They act as a vacuum cleaner to carry excess fat from the cells and tissues to the liver, which disposes of it. The higher your HDL level, the less likelihood you will develop coronary artery disease.

There is a third type of lipoproteins, known as Very Low Density Lipoproteins, (VLDL). Packets of VLDL contain little cholesterol but a lot of triglyceride, the basic type of fat used for energy storage. Though VLDL plays a role in the development of placques in arteries, its exact contribution is not yet known. This is still one of the many mysteries.

A high blood cholesterol usually reflects a high LDL. Genetic tendencies can account for some elevation, but in many people a high intake of dietary fat is responsible. You can think of your own body as being stimulated by fat to increase its production of LDL and then load cholesterol onto the carrier protein. Although dietary cholesterol somewhat elevates LDL, it has less effect than fat.

Since weight loss in obese persons can also help to lower LDL, reducing total intake of fat and calories is suggested. The water-soluble fiber in oat bran and legumes is known to lower LDL. When LDL is lowered it is usual that HDL will fall proportionately, which is exactly the opposite of what you want to achieve. The goal is to LOWER LDL and RAISE HDL.

Ordinary diet changes do not seem to affect HDL. Nothing seems to raise the level of HDL, the "Good" lipoprotein, except regular AEROBIC EXERCISE (40-60 minutes three to four times weekly), losing weight, moderating alcohol intake and not smoking. Studies have shown that AEROBIC EXERCISE on a regular basis is the key to raising HDL.

It is important that you know your
cholesterol count. EVERYONE over the
age of 20 should have a lipid panel as a
starting point. <u>BE AWARE AND KNOW</u> the
following numbers: Total cholesterol
                    LDL
                    HDL
                    Triglycerides
The ratio of HDL to total cholesterol is
important. In order to find this ratio,
divide total cholesterol by HDL. A ratio
in excess of 3.5 should raise the flag for
further evaluation.

A SOBERING THOUGHT:
Your cholesterol count may be more
important than your checkbook balance. If
you don't take cholesterol seriously, you
may not have to worry about your
checkbook.

BOTTOM LINE:
Know the facts and fight for your life!

Cut number of egg yolks in half. Use full amount of whites with maybe one extra, or use 1 egg white and 1/2 teaspoon polyunsaturated oil. (Keep in mind, an average egg yolk contains approximately 250 mg of cholesterol.)

Substitute non-fat yogurt for the oil in pancakes and waffles.

Decrease fat absorption when cooking meat or fowl by placing on a rack. Do not let sit in its own juice.

Remove all skin and excess fat before cooking meat or fowl. This reduces calories and the amount of saturated fat. It does not reduce cholesterol.

Microwave ground meat in a microwave bacon pan. Grease drains off while cooking and collects in ridges of the pan. To drain any remaining grease, place cooked meat on paper towel and refrigerate. Place in microwave on paper towel to reheat.

Avoid luncheon meats because of high fat and sodium content.

FIBER , THE BULK OF IT

Fiber plays an essential role in good
health and nutrition. It is one of the
substances we are encouraged to increase
as we consume less fat, cholesterol and
sugar. Fiber is not a single substance.
It is a catchall term for an indigestible
part of plant foods. It can be insoluble
in water, such as the fiber in wheat bran,
cereals and vegetables, or soluble, the
form found in fruits, legumes and oats.
Each fiber, with its own health ad-
vantages, has a different effect on our
bodies.

The role of fiber in the prevention of
colon cancer pointed out by many
epidemiological studies, has boosted its
popularity. Fiber bulks-up the stool and
hastens transit time through the digestive
tract. This dilutes the concentration of
carcinogens and decreases the time they
spend in contact with the colon.

Other potential benefits of increased
fiber intake are moderating high blood
pressure and lowering blood cholesterol
levels, particularly with water soluble
fibers combined with a low fat diet. In
addition, a fiber rich diet may relieve
constipation and alleviate diverticulosis.
Upping your fiber intake may also help
trim calories. This is not only a

motivational boost but a health boon to people whose weight gets them into heart and diabetes trouble.

How it works? Fiber simply takes longer to eat and to empty from the stomach, making you feel full. It may also help control insulin, an appetite stimulator. Fiber being indigestible provides virtually no calories.

There is no established recommended daily allowance (RDA) for fiber. Current recommendations vary, suggesting individuals should consume 30 to 40 grams per day. Most Americans fall short of this goal, consuming only 10 grams daily. The National Cancer Institute says it is best to get fiber from a variety of sources since each type has its own benefits. (Check the attached charts to see how your fiber intake measures up.)

While it helps to be aware of the fiber in various foods, you can insure an adequate fiber intake by gradually following these steps:
   1.   Eat a variety of foods - the less processed the better. Bran, for example, is a superb source of fiber. However, consuming it in the form of whole-grain cereals is more nutritionally sound than merely adding bran flakes as a supplement to your foods.
   2.   Eat fruits and vegetables raw when possible. They have more useful fiber than those peeled, cooked or processed.
   3.   Drink plenty of fluids. Otherwise fiber can slow, or even block digestion.
   4.   Spread your fiber intake. Getting all your fiber at one sitting may cut the benefits and increase the chance of unpleasant side effects. As a rule of thumb, have a serving of both types of fiber at every meal.

This approach will not only increase your fiber intake, but should also help lower the fat and sugar in your diet. This is another way fiber, though not a nutritional panacea, is an excellent form of health insurance.

SOBERING THOUGHT:
You should eat to live, not live to eat.

BOTTOM LINE:
Fiber contains a good deal of bulk for the calories and lends many helping hands to bodily functions.
The key to fiber intake is VARIETY.

Name:	AMT	Cal	CARBO	FAT	PRO	Gm.Fiber
Raisin Bran	3/4 C	120	83%	5%	12%	6+
Bran Buds	1/3 C	73	79%	6%	15%	6+
Corn Bran	2/3 C	62	85%	8%	7%	6+
All Bran	1/3 C	71	80%	4%	15%	6+
Wheat germ	1/4 C	108	48%	23%	28%	4+
(Toasted, plain)						
Kidney Beans	1/2 C	90	70%	0%	30%	4+
Lima Beans	1/2 C	104	76%	2%	22%	4+
Navy	1/2 C	25	63%	8%	30%	4+
Pinto	1/2 C	50	75%	3%	23%	4+
White	1/2 C	54	70%	4%	26%	4+
Popcorn	1 C	54	83%	0%	17%	1-3
Wh. Wt. Bread	1 sl.	107	86%	1%	12%	1-3
Grapenuts	1/4 C	102	87%	1%	12%	1-3
Shredded Wheat	1 lge	85	85%	3%	12%	1-3
Garbanzo Beans	1/2 C	360	66%	12%	22%	1-3
Lentils	1/2 C	105	71%	0%	29%	1-3
Almonds	10	180	13%	74%	13%	1-3
Peanuts	10	105	12%	71%	17%	1-3

Food	Serving	Cal	Carb	Fat	Protein	Fiber
Asparagus	1/2 C	17	50%	9%	40%	1-3
Green Beans	1/2 C	20	74%	5%	21%	1-3
Brussel Sprouts	1/2 C	30	70%	9%	21%	1-3
Carrots	1/2 C	35	87%	4%	9%	1-3
Green Peas	1/2 C	63	71%	3%	26%	1-3
Spinach, raw	1/2 C	90	51%	8%	41%	1-3
Tomato	1 med	30	76%	8%	16%	1-3
Apple, raw, unp.	1 med	85	95%	5%	1%	1-3
Apricot	5 half	75	93%	2%	5%	1-3
Banana	1 med	110	92%	4%	4%	1-3
Grapefruit	1/2	40	90%	2%	7%	1-3
Orange	1 med	85	91%	2%	7%	1-3
Raisins	1/4 C	108	95%	1%	4%	1-3
Strawberries	1 C	45	83%	10%	7%	1-3
Melon	1 C	60	85%	6%	9%	1-3
Blackberry	1/2 C	38	89%	6%	5%	4+
Dried Prunes	3 pcs.	100	94%	2%	4%	4+

Many foods high in fiber also supply an abundance of carbohydrate and protein and contain little or no fat. Note the exception of nuts and bran which are high in vegetable fat.

FDA Consumer - 1985
Covert Baily - On Target Data Base.

Learn to make low fat substitutions. In many instances you can CUT THE AMOUNT OF FAT IN HALF without tasting the difference.

Steaming is a great way to cook. One big pot with rack will cook vegetables, fish, etc., at the same time. Sprinkle with spices and herbs. You will be delighted with the delicate flavor while preserving as many nutrients and vitamins as possible.

Save juices, especially from fish, scallops, clams, chicken or vegetables; add spices and herbs, tomato paste or sauce, and you have a great sauce for pasta.

Use fresh garlic and onion for spice rather than garlic or onion powder or salt.

There is no benefit in substituting sea salt for regular table salt - you just pay more for the same elevated blood pressure.

MORE FOR YOUR EFFORT

Fat is the substance supplying the strongest evidence of a link between diet and cancer. Studies of human populations suggest a high fat diet increases the incidence of cancers of the breast, prostate and colon. These cancers are much less common in countries with a low fat diet.

Although eating too much of any food can result in weight gain, it is easier to gain weight eating foods higher in fat than protein or carbohydrate. Consider the time it takes to consume 1 tablespoon of mayonnaise (100 calories), in comparison to 1 large apple, also approximately 100 calories. (See comparison below.) Weight gain can lead to obesity, a risk factor in heart disease, hypertension and diabetes. Selecting a diet low in fat is naturally low in calories and high in nutrition.

Excessive fat intake not only causes obesity but also may overstimulate the gallbladder, favoring gallstone formation.

A SOBERING COMPARISON:

	APPLE	MAYONNAISE
WT. Grams	138	14
CALORIES	81	99
PROTEIN Grams	0.3	0.2
CARBOHYDRATE GM	21.1	0.4
FAT GRAMS	0.5	10
% FAT	0.5	90

(Based on 1 medium apple & 1 T mayonnaise)
(Source Pennington & Church, Food Values)

BOTTOM LINE:
Treat yourself to a LOW FAT DIET. Your body will thank you by serving you well.

Humpty Dumpty can cause us to fall
By clogging our arteries with cholesterol

When eating out, order salad dressing "on the side."

Always make sure you know what you are getting when you order from a menu. Avoid buttery and cream/cheese sauces.

For spices try Mrs. Dash (a number of salt-free varieties), Lawry's Natural Choice, New Vegit, and Herbal Seasoning-Salt Free, Low Sodium.

Reduce calories and fat by "cutting" mayonnaise with non-fat yogurt in cole slaw or salad dressings.

Watch for and AVOID palm, palm kernel and coconut oils. They are saturated fats often used in prepared mixes and processed foods since they are readily available and "the price is right." The truth is, they are expensive at any price as they can be injurious to our cardiovascular health. They are particularly insidious because they are hidden in SO MANY ITEMS. Read ingredient labels to identify.

A WINNING COMBINATION

The focus of this booklet is NUTRITION
AWARENESS and the role it plays in
maintaining or restoring cardiovascular
health and fitness. We have tried to
stress the importance of well-informed use
of nutrition information, and how it can
help uncover the HIDDEN and UNHEALTHY
quantities of FAT in foods. Before
concluding, it is important to touch on
exercise and its contribution to the
health and fitness picture.

Exercise is essential if we are to realize maximum benefit from a low-fat lifestyle. Exercise tunes and tones our bodies, increases the metabolism of the healthy foods we eat, and improves the function of our minds and bodies. It accelerates the burning of calories. If done aerobically and regularly, it draws principally from our store of fat, building muscle mass and benefiting our cardiovascular system. It reduces inches before it reduces pounds. Slowly but steadily, exercise combined with controlled fat in our diet, makes that person looking out from our mirror appear more trim. Amazingly, that shadow walking along the street soon steps with more bounce and vigor, reflecting improved energy and self-esteem.

There is no "best" form of exercise except the one you do. Variety and moderation are as important in an exercise program as they are in your diet. What, when and how are decisions you must make, and any questions should be discussed with your personal health advisor. What we do want to stress is that good nutrition alone is only half of a well-rounded program of fitness. The other half of that program is exercise. Make it fun, make it social, make it a time of contemplation- just be sure you don't make it second

place.   As we've said before, good
physical and mental health are the
greatest gifts you can give to yourself.

SOBERING THOUGHT:
Think of those who have no choice. Say
"there, but for the grace of God, go I",
and GET UP AND GO!

BOTTOM LINE:
When you reach 35 you should seriously
consider having a stress test before
undertaking an exercise program.

Make your own chips - cut corn tortillas in quarters with pizza cutter and place in 350 degree oven until crisp. (Compare when buying tortillas as some are lower in fat than others.) Also check potassium/sodium content. Remember, aim for low sodium - high potassium.

Non-Dairy substitutes frequently contain saturated fat in the form of coconut oil, palm or palm kernel oil, or hydrogenated vegetable oils, and should be avoided. These include non-dairy sour cream, non-dairy whipped toppings, frozen, aerosol powered or tubs, and non-dairy coffee creamers.

Be wary of the general term "vegetable oils"...it is often used to avoid listing the coconut, palm, and palm kernel oil.

Stay away from pre-popped popcorn as it is often prepared with palm or coconut oil. Popcorn should be popped with an air popper. For flavor, use a vegetable cooking spray and sprinkle with a non-sodium seasoning.

SOURCES

The following are all well worth the time and money. As different newsletters stress different areas, spend a little time and find the one that best suits your needs. Many publishers will send a sample copy to a prospective subscriber. It's worth the inquiry.

These publications make great gifts for the person who has every thing but good fitness habits. Many times, A WORD TO THE WISE IS SUFFICIENT!

MAGAZINES - Newsletters

AMERICAN HEALTH
P.O. Box 3016
Harlan, IA 51593-2107
$ 14.95/yearly - 10 issues

THE AEROBICS NEWS
Institute for Aerobics Research
12330 Preston Road
Dallas, TX 75230-9990
$ 20.00/yearly

Nutrition Tips
The Cooper Clinic
12200 Preston Road
Dallas, TX 75230-9990
Set of 12 - $ 14.00

American Institute for Cancer Research
Washington, D. C. 20069
Free/Accepts Donations

Tufts University Diet & Nutrition Letter
P.O. Box 2465
Boulder, CO. 80322
$ 18.00/yearly

Mayo Clinic Health Letter
Mayo Clinic
Rochester, MN 55905
$ 24.00/yearly

Harvard Medical School Health Letter
79 Garden Street
Cambridge, MA 02138
$ 15.00/yearly

The Nutrition Times
1958 Sunset Cliffs Blvd, Suite 122
San Diego, CA   92107
$ 39.00/yearly

U. C. Berkley Wellness Letter
48 Shattuck Square, Suite 43
Berkley, CA 94704
$ 15.00/yearly

Nutrition Action Newsletter
1501   16th Street N. W.
Washington, D.C.   20036
(Write for Current Price)

For the more technically oriented:

Nutrition and the M.D.
P.O. Box 2160
Van Nuys, CA 91405
$ 30.00/yearly

Additional Sources:

Many local supermarkets, hospitals,
colleges, county or state extension
services, as well as city, county or
state health departments provide free
literature for the asking.

United States Government Printing Office
Superintendent of Documents
Washington, D.C. 20402

I especially recommend HEART ATTACKS (NIH
Pub. No 86-2700) and Diet, Nutrition &
Cancer (NIH Pub. No 85-2711)
Available from:
Consumer Information Center-B (US)
P.O. Box 100
Pueblo, CO 81002
Request CONSUMER INFORMATION CATALOG

Department of Health and Human Services
Public Health Service
Food & Drug Administration
5600 Fishers Lane
Rockville, MD 20857

American Soybean Association
777 Craig
St. Louis, MO. 63141-7164

U.S. Department of Agriculture
Food and Nutrition Information Center
National Agricultural Library - Rm 304
Beltsville, MD 20705

Natl Health Info Clearing House
P.O. Box 1133
Washington, D.C. 20013

The Buying Guide for Fresh Fruits,
Vegetables, Herbs & Nuts
Blue Goose, Inc.
Educational Department
P.O. Box 1118
Hagerstown, MD 21740

United Fresh Fruit & Vegetables Assn
North Washington at Madison
Alexandria, VA   22314

Local Hospitals
Health & Nutrition Programs

Local Food Chains
Attn: Nutrition Dept.

American Heart Association
Consult your local directory.

American Cancer Society
Consult your local directory.

The following publications should be at
the top of your "WISH LIST." They provide
food for thought as well as a complete
selection of the best low-fat (HEARTFELT)
cuisine cookbooks available. Their
contents will welcome you into the
wonderful world of healthful living
through knowledge and nutrition.

THE BOOKS WITH BRACKETS CAN BE ORDERED
FROM VITAEROBICS ON THE FORM AT THE END
OF THIS SECTION. ONLY THOSE MARKED ARE
KEPT IN STOCK. If you cannot find the
others locally, please contact us.

*	Indicates cookbook/recipes
#	Indicates some recipes in connection with reading material.
F	Indicates fat content (gram) given in recipes.
C	Indicates calorie count of recipes given.

{ 1 }	$ 10.95			THE AMERICAN HEART ASSOCIATION COOKBOOK
		*	C	AMERICAN HEART ASSOCIATION Ballantine Books - 1984
{ 2 }	$ 8.95			STRETCHING ANDERSON Shelter Publications, Inc. - 1980
{ 3 }	$ 8.95			EATING WELL IN A BUSY WORLD
		*		Allen Ten Speed Press - 1986
{ 4 }	$ 5.95			FIT OR FAT Bailey Houghton Mifflin Co - 1978
{ 5 }	$ 5.95			THE FIT-OR-FAT TARGET DIET Bailey Houghton Mifflin Co. - 1984
{ 6 }	$ 5.95			TARGET RECIPES
		*		Bailey/Bishop Houghton Mifflin Co. - 1985
	$ 2.95			FOOD IS YOUR BEST MEDICINE Bieler, M. D. Ballantine Books - 1984

```
     $ 16.95    HOW TO BE YOUR OWN NUTRITIONIST
                Berger, M.D.
                William Morrow & Co., Inc. -1987
{ 7 }$  4.50    THE MIRACLE NUTRIENT Coenzyme Q10
                Bliznakov, M.D.
                Bantam Books - 1987
{ 8 }$ 12.95    JANE BRODY'S NUTRITION BOOK
                Brody
                Bantam Books - 1987
{ 9 }$ 12.95    JANE BRODY'S GOOD FOOD BOOK
        *       Living the High-Carbohydrate Way
                Brody
                Bantam Books - 1987
{ 10}$ 12.95    JEAN CARPER'S TOTAL NUTRITION
                GUIDE
                Carper
                Bantam Books - 1987
     $  8.95    BIO-NUTRIONICS LOWER YOUR
                CHOLESTEROL IN 30 DAYS
                Cheraskin, M.D. & Orenstein, Ph.D.
                Putnam Publishing Group - 1986
{ 12}$ 18.95    THE NEW AMERICAN DIET
        *       Connor
                Simon & Schuster - 1986
{ 13}$ 10.95    THE AEROBICS  PROGRAM FOR TOTAL
                WELL-BEING
                Cooper, M.D.
                Bantam Books - 1982
{ 14}$  12.95   RUNNING WITHOUT FEAR
                Cooper, M.D.
                M. Evans & Company, Inc. - 1985
{ 15}$  3.95    AEROBICS FOR WOMEN
                Cooper, Mildred
                Bantam Books - 1982
{ 16}$  9.95    THE LIVING HEART DIET
                DeBakey, Gotto, Scott, Forey
                Simon & Schuster - 1984
{ 17}$  8.95    LIGHT STYLE
                Doshi, Kidushim, Wolke
                Harper & Row - 1979
     $  16.95   MEDICAL MAKEOVER
                Geller, M. D.
                William Morrow - 1986
```

```
       $  14.95  THE GOOD FAT DIET
          #   C  Gold, M. D. & Rose-Gold
                 Bantam Books - 1987
 {18} $  10.95  EATER'S CHOICE
                 Goor, M. D. & Goor
                 Houghton Mifflin & Company - 1987
 {19} $  11.95  THE PEOPLE'S NUTRITION
                 ENCYCLOPEDIA
                 Hill, M. S., R. D.
                 Putnam Publishing Group - 1987
       $   4.95  THE FAST-FOOD GUIDE
                 Jacobson, Ph. D.
                 Workman Publishing - 1986
       $   7.95  BARBARA KRAUS COMPLETE GUIDE
                 TO SODIUM
                 KRAUS
                 New American Library - 1986
       $   5.95  THE BARBARA KRAUS CHOLESTEROL
                 COUNTER
                 KRAUS
                 Putnam Publishing Group - 1985
       $  17.95  THE K FACTOR
                 Moore, M.D., Ph.D. & Webb, Ph.D.
                 MacMillan Publishing Co.- 1986
 {20} $  11.95  THE LOWFAT LIFESTYLE
         *F-C  Parker & Gates
                 LFL Associates - 1984
 {21} $   8.95  FOOD VALUES OF PORTIONS COMMONLY
                 USED
                 Pennington, Ph.D., R.D. & Church, B.S
                 Harper & Row - 1985
 {22} $  14.95  DON'T EAT YOUR HEARTOUT COOKBOOK
           *    Piscatella
                 Workman Publishing - 1982
 {23} $   4.95  THE PRITIKIN PROMISE
                 Pritikin
                 Pocket Books - 1983
 {24} $   4.95   THE PRITIKIN PROGRAM
                 FOR DIET & EXERCISE
                 Pritikin
                 Bantam Books - 1981
 {25} $   4.95   THE PRITIKIN
                 PERMANENT WEIGHT
           *  C  LOSS MANUAL
                 Pritikin
                 Simon & Schuster-1985
```

```
{ 26} $   7.95   DELICIOUSLY LOW
         *F-C    Roth
                 New American Library - 1983
{ 27} $ 17.95    DELICIOUSLY SIMPLE
         *F-C    Roth
                 New American Library - 1986
{ 28} $   9.95   FAST & LOW
          *      Easy Recipes for Low Fat Cuisine
                 Stillman
                 Little, Brown & Company - 1985
      $ 18.50    REVERSING HEART DISEASE
                 Whitaker, M.D.
                 Warner Books, Inc. 1985
```

In case you need a little stimulation or
motivation - to help put your priorities
in order, the following will start you in
the right direction.

```
{30} $   7.95    SELF IMAGERY
                 Creating Your Own Good
                 HEALTH
                 Miller, M.D.
                 Celestial Arts - 1986
{31} $   7.95    TODAY IS MINE
                 Brownlow
                 Brownlow Publishing - 1972
{32} $   9.95    THE ROAD LESS TRAVELED
                 Peck
                 Simon & Schuster - 1978
```

TO ORDER BOOKS SEND:
Name, Address, City, State, ZIP
Telephone No.
Book title and author
Check or money order for amount of
purchase plus $ 2.00/book postage/
handling. Calif. residents add
6% sales tax to Vitaerobics, Inc.
4403 Manchester, #107,Encinitas,
Ca 92024

ORDERING INFORMATION

FAT FINDER with 64 page book <u>30% FAT...WHAT'S THAT?</u>.....$ 5.95

SHIPPING/HANDLING $1.00 for first FAT FINDER with book
$ .50 each additional

ADDITIONAL FAT FINDERS..........$ 3.95each

SHIPPING/HANDLING $ .50 for first FAT FINDER
$ .25 for each additional FAT FINDER

Organization/group inquiries are invited. Quantity discounts available.

Order Form
VITAEROBICS

4403 Manchester - #107
Encinitas, CA 92024
1-800-323-8042
(Out of CA only)

B.A. Fat Finder.

Name _____

Address _____

City _____

State _____ Zip _____

Phone # _____

Check or Money Order Payable to: *Fat Finder*™

QTY	Item	Cost EA	Total
	Sub Total		
	CA Res. Add 6% Tax		
	Shipping		
	Total		

WE WISH YOU HEALTH AND FITNESS,

Fat Composition of Oils
Percent of Total Fatty Acids

Safflower Oil
6 2 | 14 | 78

Lard
27 | 14 | 47 | 12

Sunflower Oil
6 4 | 20 | 70

Tallow
32 | 20 | 44 | 4

Soybean Oil
10 5 | 24 | 61

Butterfat
41 | 25 | 30 | 4

Corn Oil
11 2 2 | 25 | 62

Palm Oil
46 | 5 | 39 | 10

Peanut Oil
11 7 | 48 | 34

Coconut Oil
73 | 19 | 6 | 2

Cottonseed Oil
24 3 | 19 | 54

Palm Kernel Oil
75 | 11 | 12 | 2

Sources: USDA Handbook No. 8-4 and American Soybean Association.

Saturated Fats

■ Fatty acids that increase serum cholesterol levels (lauric, myristic and palmitic)

▨ Fatty acids that do not affect cholesterol levels

□ Monounsaturated

▦ Polyunsaturated